from our family to yours

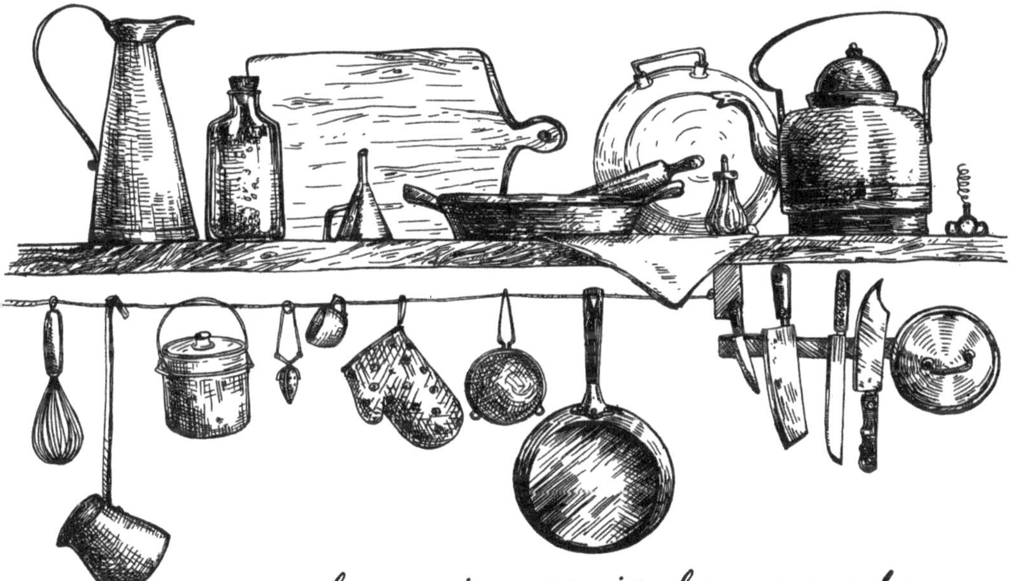

happiness is homemade

Copyright © 2023
All rights reserved.

No part of this book may be reproduced or transmitted in any form or by any means, electronic or mechanical, including photocopying, recording, or by any information storage and retrieval system, without permission in writing from the copyright owner.

Published by
GRAPH Publishing, L.L.C.
www.graphpublishing.com

Printed in the U.S.A.

Dedication Page

Acts 2: 46-47: Every day they continued to meet together in the temple courts. They broke bread in their homes and ate together with glad and sincere hearts, praising God and enjoying the favor of all the people.

    This cookbook is a collection of four plus generations of recipes from my husband's family and mine. These recipes have brought our families together for generations celebrating many holidays, birthdays, parties, and just simply quality family time together. We break bread, share stories, laugh together and make new memories that will last for many more years to come.

    I can remember as a toddler pushing a heavy chair across the tile floor making an obnoxious noise, just so I could get a glimpse of what was being prepared. Food has always been a very important part of my life. As a child I would be eating one meal asking my parents what they were going to cook me for my next meal. Those precious memories of being a child and being so excited to see what was happening in the kitchen are moments I will treasure forever. Now, as a mother of two of my own children, seeing them repeat the exact same thing by running to get their stool and rush into the kitchen begging to help cook are the precious memories I would not trade for anything. The joy that overcomes my kids when they help me cook and the huge smiles plastered across their faces as they get to eat the sweet rewards of their hard work is something I can't wait for everyone to experience in their own lives. These simple but rewarding moments together is why I want to create this cookbook of my families' recipes, so you too can experience moments like these. Family is everything, and every moment we get to share together is a priceless gift from God. So, whether you are enjoying a warm baked cookie, or a hot bowl of soup in the cold winter remember what matters, and that is family.

Table of Contents

appetizers	7
soups	17
sides and sauces	33
casseroles	59
main dishes	75
pies	103
cakes	125
cookies	149
other desserts	161
breads	181
beverages	193
canning	203

appetizers

Jalapeno Poppers

ingredients:

- 2-3 lbs. jalapenos
- 2 blocks cream cheese
- 1 lb. maple sausage
- 2 packages maple bacon
- Dry mustard
- Brown sugar

directions:

Cut the tops off the jalapeno peppers and deseed them. Brown your maple sausage in a skillet. Once cooked thoroughly add cream cheese and mix. Place cream cheese mixture into a large Ziplock bag cut one of the bottom corners off so you can pipe the mixture into the peppers. Once all the cream cheese mixture is pipped into the peppers wrap the peppers with one slice of raw maple bacon, securing the bacon with toothpicks, then place on baking sheet. Once you have wrapped all your peppers, top with a hearty helping of brown sugar and a dusting of dry mustard. Bake at 350° till bacon is cooked through. Enjoy.

Stuffed Mushrooms

ingredients:

- 2-3 containers medium portabella mushrooms
- 2 blocks cream cheese
- 5 jalapenos

directions:

Wash your mushrooms and remove the stems. Deseed and chop up your jalapenos, mix into your cream cheese. Stuff your cream cheese mixture into the mushrooms and bake at 350° till the cream cheese is browned on top.

Maple Sausage Queso Dip

ingredients:

- 2 lb Velveeta cheese block
- 1 lb maple sausage
- 1-2 cans Rotel tomatoes

directions:

Brown your maple sausage in a skillet. Mix your cooked maple sausage, cubed Velveeta, and Rotel in a crockpot. Heat, stirring occasionally. Serve with tortilla chips and enjoy.

Texas Caviar Dip

ingredients:

- 8 oz cream cheese
- 1 can black beans, drained
- 1 can Rotel tomatoes, drained
- 2 cups shredded mozzarella cheese

directions:

Spread the cream cheese in the bottom of a pie plate. Add your drained black beans, Rotel tomatoes, and mozzarella cheese. Heat in the oven at 350° till cheese melts and all is hot. Serve with Fritos corn chips.

Party Dip

ingredients:

- 1 block cream cheese, softened
- 1 cup mayo
- 3 chopped green onions
- 8 oz shredded swiss cheese
- 1/4 cup real bacon bits
- 14 ritz craackers, crushed

directions:

Mix all ingredients together, except for the crushed ritz crackers. Spread into a pie dish. Sprinkle the crushed ritz crackers over everything. Bake at 350° till hot and melted. Serve with crackers, or chips.

Curry Chicken Balls

ingredients:

- 1 block cream cheese, softened
- 2 T. orange marmalade
- 2 tsp. curry powder
- 3/4 tsp. salt
- 1/4 tsp. black pepper
- 3 cups finely chopped cooked chicken
- 3 T. finely chopped green onions
- 3 T. finely chopped celery
- 1 cup finely chopped almonds, toasted

directions:

In a large bowl, beat the first 5 ingredients until well blended. Stir in the chicken, onion and celery. Shape into 1" balls, roll in almonds. Cover and chill until firm. Serve with crackers, or decorative toothpicks.

Salad Dressing

ingredients:

    1 1/2 cups sugar
    2 T. flour
    1 cup milk
    1 egg yolk
    2 tsp. vinegar
    Salt to taste

directions:

Whisk everything together and pour over your favorite leafy green mix.

Monterey Fondue Casrole

ingredients:

12 slices of bread, crusts removed
Soft margarine
1 can cream corn
1 can green chiles
2 cups shredded jack
4 eggs slightly beaten
3 c milk
1 tsp. salt

directions:

Spread margarine on bread and cut each slice in half. Arrange half of the slices in greased baking dish, cover with half of the cream corn, half of the green chiles and half of the shredded cheese. Then repeat. Combine milk, eggs, salt, and pepper, pour over the casserole. Cover and refrigerate for 4 hours or overnight. Bake at 350° for 45-50 min or until puffy and browned.

soups

Beef Stew

ingredients:

- 2 lbs. beef stew meat
- 1 large onion chopped
- 3 stalks celery chopped
- 1 bell pepper
- 1 small bag of frozen mixed vegetables
- 1 pkg. brown gravy mix
- 2 boxes beef broth
- 3 T. Worcestershire sauce
- 2 T. minced garlic
- 1 can Rotel tomatoes
- 1/4 tsp. crushed pepper flakes
- Black pepper to taste
- Salt to taste

directions:

Brown your stew meat, remove from pot. Add in onion, bell pepper, and celery and sauté. Add your stew meat back in. In a separate bowl pour about 2 cups of your beef broth in, add in brown gravy mix, minced garlic, and all your seasonings. Whisk until well blended, pour that into your pot. Add your mixed vegetables, and Rotel tomatoes. Add in enough broth to cover all the mixture. Let simmer for about 2-4 hours. Enjoy.

Tomato Soup

ingredients:

1 qt tomatoes diced
1 cup celery chopped
1 onion chopped
1 bell pepper chopped
1 cup shredded carrots
4 tsp. minced garlic
1/4 cup butter
4 cups chicken broth
3 T. sugar
1 tsp. curry
1/4 cup flour
1/2 cup water
2 bay leaves, later removed
Salt to taste
Black Pepper to taste

directions:

Saute onion, celery, bell pepper, and carrots in butter. In a large stock pot add your sautéed vegetables, tomatoes, chicken broth, minced garlic, curry, salt, bay leaves, and black pepper. Simmer for 1 1/2 hours. After the 1 1/2 hours remove the bay leaves. In a separate bowl mix flour and water together, then add to the pot. Heat until thickens. If you want it less chunky take an emersion blender and blend until you get the consistency you desire. Serve.

The Soup

ingredients:

- 1 family size chicken and rice soup
- 1 family size ranch style beans
- 1 can cream corn
- 1 can Rotel tomatoes
- 10 oz. or more can chicken

directions:

Heat and serve over crumbled nacho cheese Doritos chips. Top with shredded cheese and green onions.

Pinto Sausage Stew

ingredients:

- 2 eckrich smoked sausage, sliced
- 4 cans jalapeno pinto beans with the juice
- 1 bell pepper
- 1 onion
- 1 can of Rotel tomatoes
- 1 can of spicy V-8 juice

directions:

Combine everything into large pot and simmer on low for 30 minutes.

Pot Of Beans

ingredients:

1-2 lbs. Dried pinto beans
Fiesta pinto bean seasoning to taste (takes a lot)
Ham hock
1 8 oz can tomato sauce
1 can Rotel tomatoes
3 boxes beef broth

directions:

Rinse your pinto beans and remove any beans that may be bad. Put your clean pinto beans into a large stock pot. Add the ham hock, tomato sauce, Rotel tomatoes, fiesta pinto bean seasoning to taste, and cover with beef broth. Simmer for 4 hours or until beans are completely soft. Adding beef broth as needed throughout the cooking process. Make sure to stir occasionally. Serve with your favorite cornbread, enjoy.

Beanie Weenies

ingredients:

    2 cans 28 oz pork n beans
    2 package all beef hotdogs
    1/2 cup brown sugar
    1/2 cup ketchup
    1/2 cup mustard

directions:

Slice up hotdogs into bite sized pieces. Mix all ingredients into large pot and heat through. Enjoy.

Potato Soup

ingredients:

6 strips of bacon
1 onion chopped
4 large russet potatoes diced
1/4 cup flour
4 cups milk
1 cup chicken broth
2 T. minced garlic
1 cup shredded cheddar cheese
Green onions chopped for garnish
3/4 cup sour cream
Black pepper to taste
Salt to taste

directions:

Cut up and fry your bacon in a large stock pot until its crispy. When bacon is done remove from the pot and add the onion to the grease and saute. Stir in flour and cook for about one minute. Whisk the milk in slowly until flour has dissolved. Add the chicken broth, garlic, and diced potatoes. Bring everything back up to a simmer and let cook for about 20 minutes. When the potatoes are soft and falling apart add the sour cream, bacon and 2/3 of the cheese. Top with green onions and serve.

Quick Potato Soup

ingredients:

    1 frozen bag O'Brien style potatoes
    1 can Rotel tomatoes
    2 cans chicken broth
Heat till done and add:
    1 pkg. white gravy mix
    2 cups Velveeta
    Salt to taste
    Black pepper to taste

directions:

Simmer till thickened, top with shredded cheese and green onions.

Casa Soup

ingredients:

- 2 lbs. hamburger meat, brown and drain
- 2 cans ranch style beans
- 1 can Rotel
- 1 pkg. ranch dressing seasoning
- 1 pkg. taco seasoning
- 1 can diced green chiles
- 1 can fire roasted tomatoes with garlic
- 2 cans water

directions:

Simmer all the ingredients for about 30 min and serve.

Cabin Soup

ingredients:

- 1 lb. hamburger
- 2 cups water
- 1 onion chopped
- 1 can stewed tomatoes
- 1 can pinto beans undrained
- 1 can veg-all undrained
- 2 cans whole white potatoes, drained and diced
- 1 pkg. sloppy joe mix
- 1 tsp. Worcestershire sauce
- Salt to taste
- Black pepper to taste

directions:

Brown hamburger meat and onion in water till tender. Yes add raw meat and chopped onion to water to cook. After meat is cooked through add all other ingredients and simmer for 30 minutes or more.

Chili

ingredients:

- 2 lbs. meat
- 1 large can red kidney beans
- 1 large can pinto beans
- 1 large can crushed tomatoes
- 2 pkg. chili seasoning
- 1 large onion chopped
- 1 bell pepper chopped
- Beef broth

directions:

Brown meat, onion and bell pepper. Add all other ingredients and add a little bit of beef broth as needed. Simmer for 2-3 hours. Top with cheddar cheese and green onions. Serve with cornbread or crackers.

Broccoli Cheese Soup

ingredients:

- 1/2 cup butter
- 1 onion chopped
- 1/2 cup flour
- 3 cups chicken broth
- 3 cups milk
- 1 T. onion powder
- 1 T. garlic powder
- 1 tsp. salt
- 1 tsp. black pepper
- 10 oz broccoli florets, chopped
- 3 cups shredded cheddar cheese

directions:

In a large stock pot saute the onion in the butter. Add the flour and cook for 3 minutes. Add the chicken broth and whisk until a thick mixture forms. Add the milk and whisk again. Stir in the seasonings. Add the chopped broccoli florets and simmer for 15 minutes. Remove from heat and add the shredded cheddar cheese, stir and serve.

Potato Corn Chowder

ingredients:

- 8 slices bacon, diced
- 2 T. butter
- 1 onion chopped
- 1/4 cup flour
- 2 T. minced garlic
- 5 cups chicken broth
- 8 ears sweet yellow corn
- 1 lb. golden potatoes
- 1/4 tsp. dried thyme
- 1/4 tsp. smoked paprika
- 1 cup half and half
- Green onions chopped
- Salt to taste
- Black Pepper to taste

directions:

Remove the corn kernels from the cob and set aside. Cook your diced bacon in a large stock pot till crispy and remove leaving the grease in the pot. Add chopped onion and saute. Add garlic and flour and cook for one minute. Whisk in chicken broth, then add in corn, diced potatoes, thyme, paprika, salt and peper. Bring to a boil the reduce the heat to medium-low heat and simmer for about 15-20 min or until potatoes are soft. Add in the half and half, bacon and half the chopped green onions. Serve with green chives and shredded cheese on top. Enjoy.

Nacho Cheese Chowder

ingredients:

- 1/2 lb. hamburger
- 1 bell bepper, chopped
- 1 can nacho cheese soup
- 1 1/4 cup milk
- 1/2 frozen corn
- 1 tsp. dried minced onion
- 1 tomato, chopped

directions:

Brown hamburger meat and bell pepper. Add all other ingredients and simmer for 20 min. Enjoy.

sides and sauces

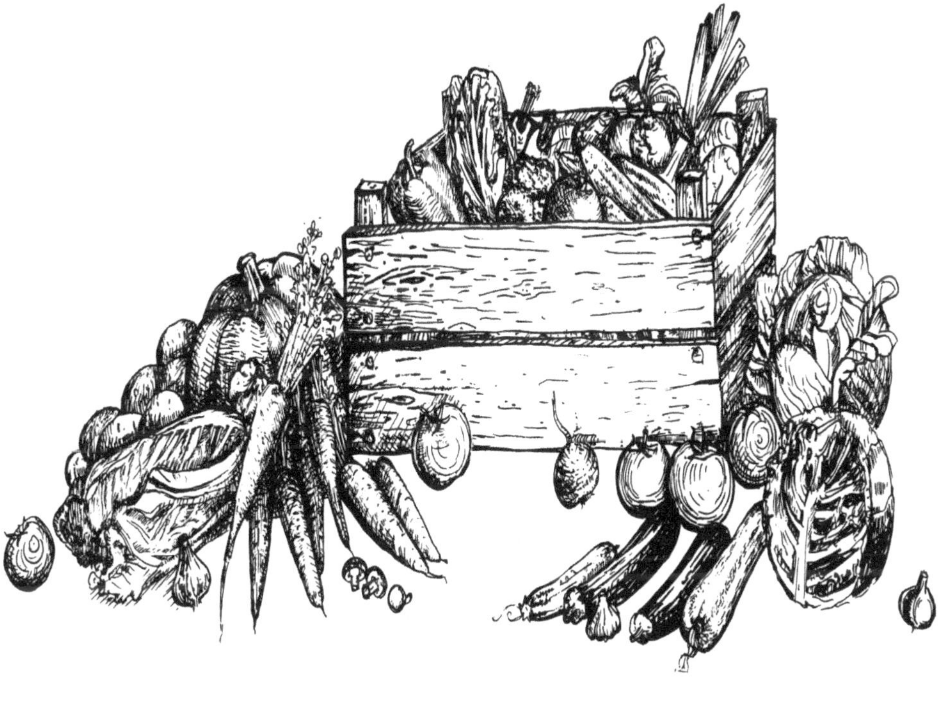

Cornbread Dressing

ingredients:

    3 boxes of cornbread
    Dried out bread, equal amount to cooked crumbled cornbread
    3 eggs
    1 1/2 cup chopped onion
    1 1/2 cup chopped celery
    Sage to taste
    Pepper to taste
    Salt to taste
    Turkey Broth

directions:

Prepare 3 packages of cornbread according to the box, and crumble. You will need equal parts chopped up dried bread to crumbled cornbread. Mix in eggs, onion, and celery. Pour in broth from turkey or boxed broth, enough to make the mixture soupy in the large baking dish. Add sage, pepper and salt to taste, give one last stir and bake at 350° for about 1 hour or until done.

Squash Dressing

ingredients:

- 2 cups cooked squash
- 1/2 stick butter melted
- 1 large onion chopped
- 2 cups crumbled cornbread
- 1 can cream chicken soup
- Salt to taste
- Black pepper to taste
- Sage if desired

directions:

Boil, drain, and mash cooked squash. Put all ingredients in dish. Bake at 400° for 30 to 40 minutes.

Hashbrown Casserole

ingredients:

- 2 lb. frozen hash browns
- 1 can chicken soup
- 1 cup sour cream
- 1 onion
- 2 cups shredded cheddar cheese
- 1 tsp. Garlic powder
- 1 tsp. Onion powder
- 1/4 tsp. Season salt
- 1 tsp. Black pepper

directions:

Mix all ingredients and bake in a greased 9x13 dish at 350° for about 40 min. Cover with foil.

Bacon Wrapped Asparagus

ingredients:

15-20 asparagus sticks
1-2 lbs. of bacon
Brown sugar
Dry mustard

directions:

Wrap each asparagus stick with one slice of bacon. Lay flat on a cookie sheet. Sprinkle a good amount of brown sugar over each bacon wrapped asparagus, and then dust with dry mustard. Bake in the oven at 350° till bacon is completely cooked.

Mexican Rice

ingredients:

1 1/2 cups uncooked white rice
2 T. oil
Minced garlic
1 large onion chopped
1 bell pepper chopped
1 8 oz. can tomato sauce
Chicken broth or water
Season salt to taste
Black pepper to taste
Onion powder to taste
Garlic powder to taste

directions:

In large skillet add your onion and bell pepper and sauté. Remove your onions and bell pepper set aside. Pour in your oil and white rice, toast your rice for about 5 min. Careful not to burn. Add minced garlic and roast for about 1 minute. Add your onion and bell peppers back into the skillet. Pour in your tomato sauce, and enough broth to fill the skillet. Stir in your seasonings. Reduce the heat to simmer and cook your rice, adding broth as needed until your rice is completely tender.

Broccoli Rice

ingredients:

- 1 pkg. frozen chopped broccoli
- 1 cup cream of chicken soup
- 2 cups white rice
- 1/2 lb. Velveeta cheese
- 1/4 cup milk

directions:

Cook rice and broccoli. Mix soup, milk and cheese together and melt. Mix together and bake 350° for 30 min.

Spinach Casserole

ingredients:

- 6 T. butter
- 8 oz white American cheese
- 6 eggs
- 6 T. flour
- 4 cups small curd cottage cheese
- 3 packages frozen spinach

directions:

Cut butter and cheese into cubes, set aside. Beat eggs, then add flour, cottage cheese, butter, and American cheese. Defrost and drain frozen spinach. Add spinach to the mixture and mix well. Put into greased dish and bake at 350° for 1 hour. Serve hot.

Warm Potato Salad

ingredients:

- 5 lbs. potatoes
- 1 large onion
- 1 jar of green olives
- Mayo
- Mustard
- Salt
- Black Pepper
- Cayenne

directions:

Wash, peel, boil, and drain the potatoes then set aside. Chop up the onion. Drain the jar of green olives and chop. In large bowl add the potatoes, onion, green olives, about 1/2 cup give or take of mayo, and about 1/4 cup mustard. Mix. Lightly break up the potatoes, leaving some chunky. You want it to be a wet mixture having more mayo than mustard. And salt and pepper to taste, and a dash of cayenne for a slight kick. Serve warm, enjoy.

Baked Beans

ingredients:

- 2 large cans pork n beans
- 1 1/2 cup brown sugar
- 1 cup Ketchup
- 1 cup Mustard
- 1 package bacon
- 1 large onion
- 2 bell peppers

directions:

Chop up your bacon into bite sized pieces and fry in skillet. When the bacon is cooked through remove it and leave the grease. Add chopped onion and bell pepper to the grease and sauté. In large baking dish add the can of pork n beans, brown sugar, ketchup, mustard, 2/3 cooked bacon, onion and bell pepper. Mix. Bake at 350° for about 1 hour, or until its no longer jiggly. 5 min before its done cooking add remaining bacon to the top.

Stuffed Tomatoes

ingredients:

- 6 large fresh tomatoes
- 1 lb. bacon
- 1 onion
- 1 sleeve crushed ritz crackers
- Salt to taste
- Black pepper to taste

directions:

Cut the stem off tomatoes, scoop out the seeds with a spoon. Slice bacon into bite size pieces and brown. Remove bacon and leave the grease to sauté the chopped onion. Combine crispy bacon, sauted onions, salt, black pepper and all but 1 cup of crushed ritz crackers. Stuff your tomatoes and top with the remaining crushed crackers and 1 pat of butter. Bake at 350° for 30 minutes.

Squash Casserole

ingredients:

- 2 lbs. yellow squash
- 1 large onion
- 2 cups cheddar cheese
- 1/2 cup heavy whipping cream
- 3 T. butter
- 1 egg
- 2 sleeves ritz crackers, crushed
- Salt to taste
- Black pepper to taste

directions:

Slice squash and chop onion. Cook in small amount of water till tender. Drain well. Put back in pan and add all ingredients, reserving 1/3 of crushed ritz crackers for the top. Pour into buttered casserole dish and add the remaining ritz crackers. Bake at 350° for 30 min.

Slaw

ingredients:

    1 pkg. Dole cabbage slaw
    1 cup almond slivered
    1 cup sun flower seeds
    1 bunched green onions
Mix all together.

Sauce:
    1/2 cup canola oil
    1/3 cup brown sugar
    1/3 cup white wine vinegar
Mix this together.

directions:

Add 2 beef ramen noodles crushed and mix all ingredients together and enjoy.

Mexican Corn

ingredients:

- 2 cans sweet corn, drained
- 2 cans cream corn
- 1 large can of diced green chiles
- 1 block cream cheese, softened
- 2 T. milk
- Black pepper to taste
- Salt to taste

directions:

In a large bowl add drained sweet corn, cream corn, green chiles, cream cheese, milk and seasonings, mix well. Pour into a baking dish and bake at 350° till bubbly and hot. Enjoy.

Scalloped Corn

ingredients:

- 1 cup sour cream
- 1 can whole sweet corn, drained
- 1 can cream corn
- 1 onion chopped
- 2 eggs
- 1 box cornbread mix
- 1 stick butter

directions:

Mix all except the butter. Pour into greased baking dish. Melt butter and drizzle over the top. Bake at 375° about 1 hour.

Pasta Salad

ingredients:

1 pkg. Italian dressing seasoning, prepared as directed
Spinach noodles
Shell macaroni
Corkscrew noodles – tri color
1 can sliced black olives, drained
1 onion chopped finely
Sliced green olives with pimento

directions:

Cook and drain all your noodles. Combine all ingredients and season with garlic salt, black pepper, natures seasoning and chill. Serve once everything is chilled.

Broccoli Salad

ingredients:

- 1 head of broccoli chopped
- 1 head of cauliflower chopped
- 1 cup mayo
- 1 cup sour cream
- 1/2 cup sugar
- 1/2 tsp. salt
- 1/2 lb. of bacon fried and crumbled
- 1 cup cheddar cheese

directions:

Mix everything together and serve.

Sweet Potato Casserole

ingredients:

- 1 stick butter
- 5-6 sweet potatoes
- 1 cup evaporated milk
- 1/2 cup milk
- 2/3 cup sugar
- 2 eggs
- 1 tsp. cinnamon

directions:

Peel, boil and mash sweet potatoes. Mix in a large bowl all ingredients. Pour into 9x13 dish and bake at 400° for 30 min. After 30 min remove from the oven and add the topping. Mix 1 cup chopped pecans, and 1/2 cup brown sugar. Sprinkle over the sweet potato casserole and bake at 250° for 10 more min.

Broccoli Cornbread

ingredients:

- 2 boxes cornbread mix
- 1 10oz box of frozen chopped broccoli (thawed)
- 1 large onion chopped
- 1 cup sour cream
- 1 cup cottage cheese
- 4 eggs
- 1 T. salt
- 1 cup cheddar cheese

directions:

Bake at 350° about 45 min in greased 9x13 pan until golden brown

Snap Green Beans and New Potatoes

ingredients:

- 2 lbs. fresh snap green beans
- 1 pkg. new potatoes
- Chicken broth
- Minced garlic
- 1 onion chopped
- Black pepper to taste
- Salt to taste

directions:

Clean and snap all your fresh green beans. Clean your new potatoes. Add everything to a stock pot and boil till new potatoes are soft. Enjoy.

Sauteed Okra

ingredients:

2 cups sliced okra
1 small onion chopped
1/2 cup flour
1 can stewed tomatoes
Salt to taste
Black pepper to taste

directions:

In large skillet mix okra, onion and flour. Saute until okra is tender. Add stewed tomatoes, salt, and black pepper. Simmer on low for 5 minutes. Enjoy.

Red Enchilada Sauce

ingredients:

- 1/4 cup oil
- 1/2 cup flour
- 4-6 cups water
- 1/2 can wolf chili
- 1 tsp. cumin
- 2 T. chili powder
- 1 T. chicken bouillon

directions:

Heat oil, stir in flour. Once a thick liquid add cumin, chili powder, and chicken bouillon. Let that fry with flour, then add the water. Stir quickly. Then add in wolf chili. Thickness will vary depending how much water you use. Simmer for about 1 hour.

Sour Cream Enchilada Sauce

ingredients:

15 oz Mexican crema sour cream
2 cans hatch green chiles with roasted garlic enchilada sauce
2 tsp. cumin

directions:

Whisk everything together. Store leftover sauce in the refrigerator.

Turkey Drippings Gravy

ingredients:

Turkey neck
Gizzards and liver from turkey
1 small onion finely chopped
Turkey broth
2 T. flour
2-3 boiled eggs chopped up

directions:

Place the turkey neck, gizzards, liver and onion in a sauce pot, cover with water and boil for about 20 min. After your done boiling it remove and discard the turkey neck. In a medium sauce pot combine chopped gizzards, chopped liver, chopped boiled eggs, turkey broth, chopped onion, and flour as needed to thicken into a gravy. Simmer till desired thickness is reached and serve over your thanksgiving turkey.

Beef Drippings Gravy

ingredients:

    2 cups juice from beef roast
    1 onion finely chopped
    1 tsp. minced garlic
    2 T. flour

directions:

Whisk all the ingredients in a medium stock pot and bring to a boil until it thickens. Serve over your beef roast.

Mexican Cornbread Casserole

ingredients:

- 2 boxes cornbread
- 1 lb hamburger meat
- 5 chopped jalapenos
- 1 can cream corn
- 1 onion
- 2 cups shredded cheddar cheese

directions:

In two separate bowls mix one bag of cornbread, half a can cream corn, and half the chopped jalapenos. Pour one bowl of the cornbread mixture into a greased 9x13 pan. Brown your meat and onion. Pour your meat on top of the cornbread mixture. Add cheese. Then pour the other bowl of cornbread mixture on top and bake at 350° until cornbread is cooked through.

Enchilada Casserole

ingredients:

- 1 lb. hamburger meat
- 1 onion
- 1 can mushroom soup
- 1 can green chiles
- 1 can enchilada sauce
- 1/2 jar picante sauce
- Chedder cheese
- Corn tortillas
- Tobacco sauce
- Salt to taste
- Black pepper to taste

directions:

Brown meat and chopped onion. Add seasoning. Mix soups, green chiles, enchilada sauce and picante sauce. Add to meat. Layer torn up tortillas, meat mixture, and cheese. Repeat till gone, and top with cheese. Bake at 350° for 30 min.

Tater Tot Casserole

ingredients:

- 1 bag frozen onion tatter tots
- 1 lb. ground beef
- 1 can cream celery soup
- 1 can golden cream of mushroom soup
- 2 tsp. dried minced onion
- Salt to taste
- Black pepper to taste

directions:

Brown your meat and drain. Add cream of mushroom soup, cream of celery soup, and seasonings to your browned meat. Pour your meat mixture into a 9x13 dish. Use your frozen tatter tots to cover the top of the meat mixture. Bake at 350° until tatter tots are golden and crispy and meat mixture is bubbly.

Chicken Tortilla Casserole

ingredients:

- Shredded longhorn cheese
- Corn tortillas
- 1-2 chickens, boiled and deboned
- 2 cans cream of chicken soup
- 1 can of cream of celery soup
- 1 can chicken broth
- 1 onion chopped
- 1-2 cans green diced chiles

directions:

Combine chicken, onion, green chiles, broth, and soups. Layer corn tortillas, chicken mixture and cheese till you have no more chicken mixture. Top with cheese and bake at 350° till heated through and bubbling on all edges.

Breakfast Casserole

ingredients:

- 1 lb. sausage
- 6 slices bread, crusts removed
- 2 cup shredded cheese
- 6 eggs
- 2 cups half and half
- 1 tsp. salt
- 1 tsp. dry mustard

directions:

Cook and drain sausage. Butter bread on both sides. Place bread in 9x13 dish. Add sausage. Top with cheese. Combine remaining ingredients and beat well. Pour over sausage. Cover and chill overnight. Remove cover and bake at 350° for 45 min.

Mexican Cheese-Wiz Casserole

ingredients:

- 1 whole chicken
- 1 can cheese-wiz
- 1 large bag nacho cheese Doritos
- 1 can Rotel tomatoes
- 1 can cream of mushroom soup

directions:

Place your whole chicken in a large stock pot and cover with water. Boil till the chicken is cooked through. Once cooked through, take the chicken out and remove the meat from the bones. In a large bowl mix Rotel, cream of mushroom soup, cheese-wiz and chicken. In a 9x13 dish layer Doritos and the chicken mixture, repeat until the chicken mixture is gone. Bake at 350° until heated through and bubbly. Enjoy.

Omelette Casserole

ingredients:

6 eggs
1/2 tsp. onion powder
1/2 tsp. salt
1/2 tsp. black pepper
1 pkg. frozen shredded hash browns, thawed
1 cup shredded swiss cheese
1/2 cup diced cooked ham
1 can green chiles
1 cup sour cream

directions:

Beat eggs and seasoning well. Stir in other ingredients. Pour into greased pie plate and bake at 350° for 45 min or till set.

Zucchini Hamburger Casserole

ingredients:

- 1 lb. zucchini, sliced
- 1 lb. hamburger meat, cooked
- 1 1/2 cup instant rice, cooked
- 1 can golden mushroom soup
- 4 oz. sliced velveeta
- 2 1/2 cup stewed tomatoes

directions:

Place 1/2 the zucchini in the baking dish. Add in layers meat, rice, soup, the rest of the zucchini, cheese and tomatoes. Bake at 350° for 1 1/2 hour or till bubbly and tender.

Mexican Casserole

ingredients:

Brown and drain:
    1 lb. hamburger
    1 onion chopped

Add:
    2 T. chili powder
    2 cans Rotel tomatoes
    1 can jalepeno pinto beans
    2 cups minute tice, uncooked
    Salt to taste
    Black pepper to taste

directions:

Brown your meat and onion then drain. Mix in all the ingredients and pour into 9x13 baking dish, cover and bake at 350° for 5 min. or until rice is cooked through. Top with cheese and serve.

Jalapeno Chicken and Rice Casserole

ingredients:

- 2 cups cooked rice
- 2 cups shredded monterey jack cheese
- 1 1/2 cups cooked chicken
- 1 can reduced fat evaporated milk
- 1/2 cup chopped red onion
- 2 large eggs, lightly beaten
- 1/4 cup chopped cilantro
- 2 T. butter, melted
- 1 T. diced jalapenos
- Salt to taste
- Black pepper to taste

directions:

Combine chicken, cheese, rice, evaporated milk, onion, eggs, cilantro, butter, salt, black pepper and jalapenos in a 9x13 baking dish. Bake at 350° for 45-50 min. or until bubble and heated through. Enjoy.

Chicken Broccoli Casserole

ingredients:

- 2 pkg. 10 oz frozen broccoli
- 2 cups cooked chicken, chopped
- 2 cans cream of chicken soup
- 1 cup mayonnaise
- 1 tsp. lemon juice
- 1/8 tsp. curry powder
- 1 lb. shredded cheese

directions:

Cook your broccoli and drain. Place cooked chicken on top of the broccoli. Mix soup, mayonnaise, lemon juice, curry powder and pour over you chicken. Cover with shredded cheese. Bake at 350° for 30-35 min. Serve with rice or mashed potatoes.

Chicken Cornbread Casserole

ingredients:

- 4 cups crumbled cornbread
- 1/4 cups chopped green bell peppers
- 1/4 cup chopped onion
- 1/4 tsp. poultry seasoning
- Salt to taste
- Black pepper to taste
- 3 cups chopped cooked chicken
- 1 can cream of chicken soup
- 2 cups chicken broth
- Paprika if desired

directions:

Combine crumbled cornbread, bell pepper, onion and seasonings. Place half the mixture in a 2 qt. baking dish. Spread chicken over cornbread layer. Combine soup and broth, pour over chicken and cornbread. Add remainder of cornbread mix over chicken. Press down. Set aside for 20 min. Sprinkle on paprika. Bake at 350° for 30 min.

Chicken Casserole

ingredients:

- 2 boneless chicken breasts
- 1 can french style green beans
- 1 can cream of mushroom soup
- 1/2 lb. Velveeta cheese
- 1 small pkg. sliced almonds

directions:

Boil the chicken breast and chop. In a sauce pan mix soup and cubed velveeta cheese. Heat on medium until cheese is melted, stirring continuously. Do not add water. Spray 8x8 baking dish with spray oil. Drain green beans. Mix everything into the baking dish and top with almonds. Bake 20-30 min. at 350° until bubbly.

Quick Chicken Casserole

ingredients/directions:

    4 cans chunk white chicken
Crumble the chicken in a 9" square baking dish.

Mix:
    1 can cream of mushroom soup
    1 cup sour cream
Pour over chicken. Crush one sleeve of saltine crackers and spread over soup mix. Drizzle 1 stick melted butter over everything. Bake at 325° about 25 min.

main dishes

Beef Pot Roast

ingredients:

- 2-3 lbs. beef roast
- 1 large onion
- 1 lb. carrots
- 5 sticks of celery
- Minced garlic
- 2-3 boxes beef broth
- 3 pkgs brown gravy mix
- Season salt
- Onion powder
- Garlic powder
- Black pepper

directions:

In large dutch oven brown your roast on all sides using a little bit of oil. Chop onion, and celery. Peel carrots leaving them whole. Add to the browned roast. In separate bowl whisk 1 box of broth, 3 pkgs of brown gravy mix, minced garlic and seasonings. Pour over meat. Top with remaining broth as needed throughout the cooking process. Place the lid on the dutch oven and cook in the oven at 375° for about 2-3 hours then lower the temperature to 350° for the remaining 2-3 hours. Cooking in total for about 6+ hours. Serve with mashed potatoes and rolls.

12 Hour Beef Roast

ingredients:

3 lb. chuck roast
1 lb. dry pinto beans (checked and washed)
1 onion
1 can Rotel
1 can green chiles
2 8 oz cans tomato sauce
Salt to taste
Black pepper to taste

directions:

Place roast in a dutch oven. Add beans. Mix all other ingredients in a separate bowl and then pour over the meat and beans. Add water to water to within 2" from the top. Cover with lid and bake at 250° for 12 hours. Uncover, stir and bake a cook a little longer.

Deep Fried Turkey

ingredients:

12 lb. whole turkey (completely thawed)
Peanut oil (enough oil for your outdoor turkey fryer)
Tony Chachere's Creole Butter Injection
Season salt
Paprika
Cayenne
Onion powder
Garlic powder
Black pepper

Make sure your turkey is completely thawed!

directions:

Gather your turkey fryer and place it outside away from your house or any trees. Fill your fryer with the peanut oil about 2/3 the way full. Don't fill the oil all the way up, when you place your turkey in the oil the level of the oil will rise! Turn the heat on and get the oil heating up. While the oil is heating up go inside and prepare your turkey. Place your thawed turkey on the hook for the fryer. Prepare and inject your Tony Chachere's Creole Butter according to the instruction on the bottle. Once your turkey is injected you will season the top of the skin. There is no right or wrong way to do this, you just start sprinkling of all of your seasonings on, make sure to coat every inch of the bird. Once you have covered your bird in the seasoning you are ready to fry the turkey. Go check your oil temp outside it should be at 350°, once your oil is to temp you can slowly place your turkey into the oil. Cook your turkey about 3 1/2 minutes per pound, or until a meat thermometer reads an internal temperature of 180°. Bring your cooked turkey inside and let it rest for 5 min then carve and enjoy.

Glazed Ham

ingredients:

- 10 lb. bone in ham
- 1 small jar of whole cloves
- Pinch of ground cloves
- 2/3 cup brown sugar
- 1 can pineapple rings with juice
- 1/2 tsp. garlic powder
- 1/2 tsp. onion powder

directions:

Place the ham in a large roaster pan. Take your whole cloves and poke them into the skin all over the ham. Mix in a bowl pineapple juice, brown sugar, garlic powder, onion powder and pinch of ground cloves. Brush some of the glaze on the ham, reserving some to brush on throughout the duration of the cooking time. Use toothpicks and pin the pineapple rings all over the ham, using all the pineapple rings. Bake according to the heating directions on the ham.

Oven Tender Brisket

ingredients:

3 lb. beef brisket
2 pkgs. Lipton onion soup mix

directions:

Wrap your beef brisket in foil and sprinkle on lipton onion soup mix. Make sure to wrap it up tightly, to lock in all the moisture. Place in large roaster pan with lid. Bake in the oven at 250° for 8-10 hours.

Sweet and Savory Crockpot Brisket

ingredients:

- 1 beef brisket 3-3 1/2 lbs. cut in half
- 1 cup catsup (ketchup)
- 1/4 cup grape jelly
- 1 pkg. lipton onion soup mix
- 1 bell pepper chopped

directions:

Mix ingredients. Place half the brisket in crockpot. Spread half of the mix on the meat. Repeat. 8-10 hours on low.

Meatloaf

ingredients:

- 3 lbs ground beef
- 2-3 large Bell peppers
- 1-2 large Onions
- 1 Sleeve of crackers
- 2 eggs
- 1 large can tomato sauce
- 1 T. Season salt or to taste
- 2 T. Onion powder
- 2 T. Garlic powder
- 1 T. black pepper or to taste

directions:

Dice up onions and 1-2 bell peppers, leave one bell pepper for the topping. In large bowl mix (using your hands) the meat, chopped up onions and bell peppers, eggs, all the seasonings, 1/2 the sleeve of crackers, 2/3 can of tomato sauce. Add more crackers as needed, careful not to make it too dry. Form the meat mixture into a loaf in the baking dish. Using the side of your hand press a trough into the top of the meatloaf. Pour remaining tomato sauce into the trough. Slice the bell pepper you set aside into pretty rings and place the rings over the top of the meatloaf. Bake at 350° for about 1 hour or until cooked all the way through.

Easy Meatloaf

ingredients:

- 2 lb. hamburger meat
- 1 pkg. lipton onion soup mix
- 3/4 cup bread cumbs
- 2 eggs
- 3/4 cup water
- 1/3 cup ketchup

directions:

Mix all ingredients into a loaf shape. Make a dent, long ways, to help with the baking.

For the top mix 1 cup brown sugar and 1/2 cup ketchup then spread over the top of the loaf. Bake at 350° for 1 hour.

Stuffed Bell Pepper Skillet

ingredients:

- 1 lb. ground beef
- 2 bell peppers chopped
- 1 large onion chopped
- 2 packages of minute brown rice with quinoa
- 1/4 Worcestershire sauce
- 2 T. lime juice
- 1 can green enchilada sauce
- 1 can Rotel tomatoes
- 1 T. cumin
- Salt to taste
- Black pepper to taste
- Broth as needed for rice

directions:

Brown ground beef. Sauté chopped onion, and chopped bell pepper. Mix into meat. Add remaining ingredients and simmer until rice is soft adding broth as needed. Top with shredded cheese and serve with tortilla chips.

Stuffing Crusted Chicken Pot Pie

ingredients:

- 2 lbs diced chicken breast
- 1 large onion chopped
- 1 bag frozen mixed vegetables
- 1 can cream of mushroom soup
- 1 can cream of chicken soup
- 2 boxes stovetop chicken stuffing
- Salt to taste
- Black pepper to taste

directions:

Dice and cook your chicken breast. Sauté your chopped onion. Cook the two boxes of stovetop stuffing according to the box. Set aside. Mix your chicken, onion, cream of mushroom soup, cream of chicken soup, frozen vegetables, salt and pepper. Pour your chicken mixture into a 9x13 baking dish and top with your prepared stovetop stuffing making sure to cover all the chicken mixture. Bake at 350° till all the sides are bubbling. Enjoy.

Creamy Meatballs

ingredients:

- 2-3 lbs. ground beef
- 2 cans cream mushroom soup
- Garlic powder to taste
- Salt to taste
- Black pepper to taste
- 6 eggs beaten
- Seasoned bread crumbs
- Oil

directions:

In large bowl mix your raw ground beef, garlic powder, salt, and back pepper together. Form your meatballs. Dip one meatball at a time into the beaten eggs then roll it in the seasoned bread crumbs. Fry in a skillet with a little bit of oil till completely cooked through. Add your cooked meatballs to a baking dish and smother with the cream of mushroom soup. Bake at 350° until warm and bubbly.

Sweet and Sour Meatballs

ingredients:

- 16 oz whole cranberry sauce
- 12 oz chili sauce
- 1 T. brown sugar
- 1 T. mustard
- 1 T. lemon juice
- 2 cloves garlic minced
- 1 large bag of frozen meatballs

directions:

Heat cranberry sauce, chili sauce, brown sugar, mustard, lemon juice, and garlic in pan. Put bag of the frozen meatballs into crockpot to thaw. Pour the heated sauce over the thawed meatballs. Keep on low and enjoy.

Shepards Pie

ingredients:

- 3 lbs. golden potatoes
- 2 lbs. ground beef
- 1 pkg. brown gravy mix
- 1 family size can tomato soup
- 2 cups frozen mixed vegetables
- 1 box beef broth
- 1/4 cup Worcestershire sauce
- 1 large onion chopped
- Garlic powder to taste
- Onion powder to taste
- Black pepper to taste
- Salt to taste

directions:

Wash, boil and mash your golden potatoes. Set aside. Brown your meat and onion. Add in your frozen mixed vegetables, Worcestershire sauce, seasonings, brown gravy mix, and tomato soup. Mix well. Add in enough beef broth to make it a little soupy. Pour your meat mixture into a 9x13 baking dish and top with your mashed potatoes. Bake at 350° until its bubbling on all the edges and the potatoes are golden.

Beef On A Bun

ingredients:

- 1 bottle of catsup (ketchup)
- 3 tsp. mustard
- 2 tsp. brown sugar
- 1 T. Worcestershire sauce
- 3 tsp. liquid smoke
- 1 tsp. salt
- 1/2 tsp. red pepper flakes
- 2 tsp. garlic salt
- 1 – 1 1/2 lbs. of meat

directions:

Brown your meat. Mix all ingredients together and simmer for 5-10 minutes. Scoop onto hamburger buns and enjoy.

Impossible Quiche

ingredients/directions:

Butter a 9" or 10" pie plate- set aside.
- Put 1/2 lb. bacon, crisp and crumbled in pie plate.
- 1 cup shredded swiss or cheddar cheese
- 1/2 cup chopped onion
- 1/2 chopped bell pepper
- 1/2 cup chopped or sliced mushrooms

Spread ingredients evenly.

Blend at high speed in blender:
- 4 eggs
- 2 cups milk
- 1/2 Bisquick
- 1/4 tsp. salt
- 1/8 tsp. pepper

Blend 1 minute and pour into pie plate.

Bake at 350° until golden brown and custard is set. 50-55 min. Let stand 5 min, cut and serve.

Poppyseed Chicken

ingredients:

- 8 chicken breasts, boiled and diced up
- 8 oz. low fat sour cream
- 2 cans cream of chicken soup
- 2 cups crushed ritz crackers
- 2 T. poppyseed
- 1/4 tsp. garlic salt
- 1/4 tsp. dried chopped onion
- 1 stick margarine melted

directions:

Cut up chicken, mix all ingredients reserving 1/2 crushed ritz crackers. Pour into 9x13 casserole dish, top with remaining ritz crackers and melted butter. Bake at 350° for 40 minutes.

Chicken Spaghetti

ingredients:

- 6 chicken breasts
- 1 large onion
- 3-4 celery stalks
- 1 T. oil
- 1 can cream muchroom soup
- 1 pt. half and half
- 2 cups shredded cheddar cheese
- Garlic salt to taste
- Black pepper to taste
- 1/2 cup parmesan
- 1 1/2 lbs. spaghetti noodles

directions:

Cook chicken breasts in water and dice. In huge skillet sauté chopped onion and chopped celery stalks in oil till tender. Add can mushroom soup, half and half, cheddar cheese, garlic salt, black pepper, parmesan and a little chicken broth. Cook broken spaghetti noodles in remaining chicken broth. Combine chicken, noodles, and sauce in 9x13 pan. Bake at 350° till bubbly.

Baked Spaghetti

ingredients:

- 1-2 lbs. ground beef
- 1 large onion chopped
- 1 6 oz can tomato paste
- 2 tsp. chili powder
- 1 jar spaghetti sauce
- 1 box of spaghetti noodles
- 2 cups grated parmesan cheese

directions:

Brown ground beef and chopped onion. Add tomato past and chili powder. Cook the box of noodles till almost done, drain. In large bowl mix meat mixture, jar of spaghetti sauce, and noodles. Pour into 9x13 baked dish and cover with grated parmesan cheese. Bake at 350° till cheese is melted and sauce is bubbling.

Easy Lasagna

ingredients:

- 30 oz. ricotta cheese
- 2 cups shredded mozzarella
- 1/2 cup or more grated parmesan cheese
- 2 eggs
- 1 jar Bertolli tomato basil sauce
- 1 jar Bertolli Alfredo sauce
- 12 uncooked lasagna noodles
- 1 lb. hamburger

directions:

Combine ricotta, mozzarella, 1/2 parmesan, and eggs in large bowl. Combine sauces in medium bowl. Brown meat. Spread 1 cup sauce in 9x13 pan. Layer 4 uncooked lasagna noodles, sauce, cheese mixture, meat. Repeat till all is used. Sprinkle on remaining parmesan cheese. Cover with foil. Bake at 375° for 1 hour. Remove foil and bake 10 more minutes. Let stand 10 minutes and serve.

Oven Fried Pork Chops

ingredients:

- 4 pork chops trimmed
- 2 T. butter melted
- 1 egg beaten
- 2 T. milk
- 1/4 tsp. black pepper
- 1 cup stuffing mix

directions:

Pour butter into 9x13 pan. Put stuffing mix in bag and crush. Mix milk, egg and black pepper together in bowl. Dip pork chops into egg mixture. Then coat with crushed stuffing mix. Place in buttered pan. Bake at 425° for 10 minutes, turn pork chops and bake for additional 10 minutes, or until all pink is gone and juices run clear.

Mexican Ranch Chicken

ingredients:

- 2 lbs. chicken breast
- 1 pkg. spicy ranch seasoning
- 1 15 oz. can black beans, drained
- 1 15 oz. can sweet corn, drained
- 1 can Rotel tomatoes
- 1 can diced green chiles
- 1 block cream cheese
- 1 onion chopped

directions:

In a slow cooker place your whole, raw chicken breast on the bottom. Cover your chicken breast with the spicy ranch seasoning, sweet corn, black beans, Rotel tomatoes, chopped onion, and green chiles. Then place your block of cream cheese right on top. Put your lid on and cook on low for 6-8 hours or high for 4 hours. Once your chicken is cooked through, use two forks and shred the chicken in the slow cooker. Stir everything together and serve.

Sour Cream and Bacon Crockpot Chicken

ingredients:

- 8 bacon slices
- 1/3 cup diced onions
- 4 boneless chicken breasts
- 1 can cream chicken soup
- 1 can cream of mushroom soup
- 1 cup of sour cream
- 1/2 tsp. garlic powder
- Salt to taste
- Black pepper to taste

directions:

Slice each chicken breast in half and wrap one slice of bacon around it securing the bacon with a toothpick. Place the wrapped chicken in the crockpot. Sprinkle the diced onion on top. In large bowl whisk remaining ingredients and pour over chicken. Cook on low for 5-6 hours. Remove toothpicks from the chicken and place the chicken on a platter. Stir the sauce in the crockpot and pour over the chicken.

Serve over rice, egg noodles, or mashed potatoes.

Mystery Chicken

ingredients:

- 4 chicken breasts
- 1 cup apricot jam
- 1 pkg. lipton onion soup mix
- 1 cup bottled Italian salad dressing

directions:

Put chicken in shallow dish. Mix the rest of the ingredients together and pour over the chicken. Bake uncovered at 325° for 1 hour.

Cheese Chicken and Rice

ingredients:

- 1 can cream of chicken soup
- 1 1/3 cup water
- 3/4 cup uncooked minute rice
- 2 cup fresh or frozen vegetables
- 1/2 tsp. onion powder
- 1/2 tsp. black pepper
- 4 boneless chicken breasts
- 1 cup cheese

directions:

Stir soup, water, rice, vegetables and seasoning in a 8x12 shallow dish. Top with chicken breasts. Cover and bake at 375° for 45 min or until done. Top with cheese and melt.

Paprika Chicken

ingredients/directions:

    1-2 lbs. diced chicken breasts
    1 pkg. lipton onion soup mix
    1 1/2 cups water

Add all the ingredients above to the chicken in the skillet. Cook 20 min in 350° oven covered. Remove from oven and add:

    1 stick butter
    4 T. paprika
    3 T. sugar

Scrape up the browned chicken pieces from the bottom of the skillet using ingredients above. Add 1 cup heavy whipping cream to skillet and cook another 10-15 min in the oven.

Smoked Sausage Bake

ingredients:

- 1 lb. Eckrich smoked sausage sliced
- 2 yellow squash
- 2 green zuchinni
- 1 pkg. cherry tomatoes
- 4 diced potatoes
- 1 onion chopped
- 1 bell pepper chopped
- Season salt to taste
- Black pepper to taste

*You can use whatever vegetables you like.

directions:

Prepare all the ingredients and lay evenly on a large cookie sheet, drizzle with olive oil. Add your seasoning. Bake at 350° till everything is soft and cooked through, stirring once during the cooking process.

pies

Perfect Pie Crust

ingredients:

Mix:
- 4 cup flour
- 1 3/4 cup Crisco, use 2 butter knives to "cut" in Crisco
- 1 T. sugar
- 2 tsp. salt

Mix:
- 1 egg
- 1 T. vinegar
- 1/2 cup water

directions:

Makes 4 pie crusts.

Mix egg, vinegar and cup water. Add to flour mixture and mix well. Form into 4 crusts (don't roll flat until you are ready to use). You can also wrap each crust ball in wax paper and freeze. Use one of the four crusts for one pie dish.

Simple Pie Crust

ingredients:

    2 cup flour
    1/2 cup shortening
    5 T. water
    1 T. vinegar
    1 egg

directions:

Makes 1 pie crust.

Sift flour and mix all the ingredients together. Roll out and lay into your pie dish. Fill with our choice of filling.

Key Lime Pie

ingredients:

9" graham cracker crust.
Filling:
- 14 oz. sweetened condensed milk
- 3 egg yolks
- 1/2 cup key lime juice

Cool Whip:
- 1 1/2 cups Heavy whipping cream
- Sugar, to taste

directions:

Filling:
Mix all ingredients and bake at 350° for 15 min. let cool, then refrigerate.

Cool Whip:
In a bowl beat the heavy whipping cream and sugar until thick, stiff and creamy. You need to be able to form peaks without them falling. Spread over cold pie and serve.

Pecan Pie

ingredients:

- 3 eggs beaten
- 3/4 cup sugar
- 3/4 cup white karo
- 3 T. melted butter
- 1 tsp. vanilla
- 1 tsp. white vinegar
- 1/8 tsp. salt
- 2 cups chopped pecans

directions:

Mix all of the ingredients well, except for the pecans. Stir in pecans. Pour into unbaked pie shell. Bake at 350° for about 1 hour till puffy and set.

Peanut Butter Pie

ingredients:

Makes 2 pies. Make and bake two pie crusts ahead of time, or use two graham cracker crusts.

- 2/3 cup powdered sugar
- 1/3 cup peanut butter

Mix the above ingredients until it crumbles.

- 1 large pudding mix*

directions:

Mix your chocolate or vanilla instant pudding mix according to the box. Take 1/2 the peanut butter crumble mixture put in the bottom of the pie dish, then add your pudding. Add the other 1/2 of the peanut butter crumble mixture on top of the pudding. Top the pie off with cool whip, refrigerate.

*If you use a small box of pudding mix instead of large box you can make one chocolate pudding pie and one vanilla pudding pie.

Jif Peanut Butter Pie

ingredients:

9" chocolate cookie pie crust

- 1 cup creamy Jif peanut butter
- 1/2 cup sugar
- 8 oz. cream cheese, room temp
- 12 oz. cool whip tub
- 1 jar hot fudge topping

directions:

Combine Jif peanut butter, sugar, and cream cheese. Fold in 3 c. of cool whip. Spoon onto pie crust. Microwave the hot fudge for 1 min. and spread over the pie carefully. Chill. Top with remaining cool whip. Chill. Enjoy.

Lemon Muringue Pie

ingredients:

1 baked pie crust or graham cracker crust.

1/2 cup lemon juice
1 tsp. lemon rind (optional)
1 15 oz can sweetened condensed milk
2 eggs- separated
1/4 tsp cream of tartar
4 T. sugar

directions:

Combine lemon juice and rind, stir into sweetened condensed milk. Add egg yolks and stir till blended. Pour into chilled crust.

Meringue:

Add cream of tartar to egg whites, beat until about stiff enough to hold a peak. Add sugar gradually beating till stiff but not dry. Pile lightly on pie filling. Bake at 325° until lightly browned about 15 min. Cool.

Custard Pie

ingredients:

Pastry for 9" shell.

- 3 large eggs
- 3/4 cup sugar
- 2 1/3 cup milk
- 1/2 tsp. salt
- 1/4 tsp. nutmeg
- 1 tsp. vanilla

directions:

Beat eggs slightly, then beat in vanilla, nutmeg, salt, sugar, and milk. Pour into chilled shell. Bake at 450° for 10 min. and reduce heat to 350° and bake another 30 min.

Strawberry Pie

ingredients:

9" graham cracker crust

1 1/2 cup sugar
1 1/2 cup water
1/2 cup cornstarch
1 box strawberry Jello mix
Fresh strawberries sliced

directions:

Cook sugar, water and cornstarch till thick and clear. Add Jello mix. Stir in strawberry slices. Fills 1 large graham cracker crust or 2 small crusts. Chill and top with cool whip.

Ritz Cracker Pecan Pie

ingredients:

- 1 cup ritz crackers
- 1 1/2 cups chopped pecans
- 3 egg whites, beaten stiff
- 1 cup sugar
- 1 tsp. baking powder
- 1 tsp. vanilla
- 1 8oz cool whip tub

directions:

Crush the ritz crackers in a bag. In a large mixing bowl beat the egg whites until stiff. Add the sugar and mix. Add the baking powder and vanilla and mix again. Fold in crushed crackers and chopped pecans. Pour into greased pie dish and bake at 350° for 25-30 minutes. Let cool completely. Serve with a dollop of cool whip, enjoy.

Cinnamon Roll Apple Pie

ingredients:

Crust:
    2 cans cinnamon rolls

Pie filling:
    6 granny smith apples peeled, cored, and sliced thin
    2 T. flour
    1 1/4 tsp. pie spice
    2 T. lemon juice

Mix the ingredients above and pour over sliced apples. Coat your apples completly.

Crumb topping:
    1 cup flour
    1 cup brown sugar
    1/2 cup butter

directions:

Open your cinnamon rolls, roll out each cinnamon roll flat with a rolling pin. Lay them out flat in a buttered pie dish. Make sure to go up the edges of the pie dish with the cinnamon rolls. Fill with apple mixture.

Mix crumb topping in bowl and crumble over top of the pie. Or you can use more flattened cinnamon rolls as a top crust. Bake at 375° for 1 hour, make sure all cinnamon rolls are done. Enjoy.

Apple Pie

ingredients:

6 granny smith apples, peeled, cored, sliced thin
1 cup sugar
2 T. flour
Dash salt
1 tsp. cinnamon
1/4 tsp. nutmeg

directions:

Mix everything together and pour over sliced apples. Coat your apples completly. Fill your pie crust evenly. Dot with butter. Add top crust. Sprinkle with sugar and cinnamon. Bake at 400° about 50 min.

Fried Mini Pies

ingredients:

　　2 cans of ready biscuits
　　Oil
　　Strawberry jam
　　Blackberry jam
　　Apple sauce
　　Powdered sugar

You can use any flavor jam you have!

directions:

Get a medium size sauce pot and pour enough oil to fry your pies in. Turn the heat onto medium high. Open your ready biscuits and roll each one out flat. On one half of the flattened biscuit put a good size spoonful of your choice of jam or apple sauce. Fold over the biscuit to form a pocket to hold in your filling of choice. Then use a fork to crimp the edges so your filling doesn't ooze out. Carefully place your pies into the oil and cook until golden brown. Remove from the oil and sprinkle powdered sugar on top of your pies. Enjoy.

*If you don't want to fry your pies you can also bake them. Prepare the pies the same way then place your pies on a sheet pan and bake them at 350° until golden brown. Top with powdered sugar and enjoy!

French Lemon Pie

ingredients:

    1 cup sugar
    2 T. flour
    1/4 cup lemon juice
    1 T. butter
    4 eggs
    Pinch of salt

Whip Cream:
    1 1/2 cups heavy whipping cream
    Sugar to taste

directions:

In a large bowl beat all the ingredients and pour into a pie crust. Bake at 350° for 50 min.

In a seprate bowl beat heavy whipping cream and sugar, to taste, until thick, stiff and creamy, you need to be able to form peaks. Spread onto cooled lemon pie and serve. Enjoy.

Pumpkin Pie

ingredients:

Crust: Makes 4 pie crusts.
- 4 cup flour
- 1 3/4 cup Crisco
- 1 T. sugar
- 2 tsp. salt

Mix using 2 butter knives to "cut" in Crisco. Mix 1 egg, 1 T. vinegar and 1/2 cup water. Add to flour mixture and mix well. Form into 4 crusts (don't roll flat until you are ready to use). You can also wrap each crust ball in wax paper and freeze. Use one of the four crusts for one pie dish.

Filling:
- 3/4 cup sugar
- 1 tsp. cinnamon
- 1/2 tsp. ginger
- 1/4 tsp. cloves
- 2 eggs
- 1 15oz can pumpkin puree
- 1 can evaporated milk

directions:

Mix sugar, cinnamon, salt, ginger and cloves in small bowl. In a separate bowl beat the eggs. Then add in the can of pumpkin puree, and sugar-spice mixture. Gradually stir in the evaporated milk. Pour into one of your prepared uncooked pie crusts. Bake at 425° for 15 minutes. Then reduce the temperate to 350° and bake for 40 minutes or until set. Cool completely and enjoy.

Chiffon Pumpkin Pie

ingredients:

Crust:
- 2 cup flour
- 1/2 cup shortening
- 5 T. water
- 1 T. vinegar
- 1 egg

Sift flour and mix all the ingredients together. Roll out and lay into your pie dish.

Filling:
- 1 cup pumpkin puree
- 2 egg yolks beaten
- 1 cup scalded milk
- 1 T. melted butter
- 1/2 cup sugar
- 1/2 cup brown sugar
- 1/2 tsp. salt
- 1/2 tsp. cinnamon
- 1/2 tsp. nutmeg
- 1/2 tsp. ground mace
- 2 egg whites beaten stiff

directions:

Mix everything together and pour over sliced apples. Coat your apples completly. Fill your pie crust evenly. Dot with butter. Add top crust. Sprinkle with sugar and cinnamon. Bake at 400° about 50 min.

Cherry Cream Cheese Pie

ingredients:

10" graham cracker crust

    8 oz cream cheese, room temp
    1 can sweetened condensed milk
    1/3 cup lemon juice
    1 tsp. vanilla
    1 can cherry pie filling

directions:

Beat the cream cheese till fluffy. Add in sweetened condensed milk and mix well. Blend in lemon juice and vanilla. Pour into pie crust and chill for 2-3 hours. Top with cherry pie filling. Enjoy.

Plum Tort Pie

ingredients:

Filling:
- 2 lbs plums sliced thin
- 1/2 cup sugar
- 1 T. lemon juice
- 4 tsp. cornstarch
- 1/2 tsp. salt

Crumb topping:
- 12 T. butter room temp.
- 1/2 cup brown sugar
- 2 cups flour
- 1/2 tsp. salt

directions:

Slice plums thin, stir in sugar, lemon juice, salt, and cornstarch place in pie dish. Beat butter, brown sugar then add flour and salt. Gather small handfuls of the mixture and squeeze to clump, then lightly break apart over pie filling. Bake at 375° for 30 min. then cover loosely with foil and bake another 20 min until filling is bubbling and topping is brown.

Cherry Pie

ingredients:

2 9" pie crust, unbaked

- 3/4 cup to 1 cup water
- 3/4 cup sugar
- 2 T. cornstarch
- Pinch of salt
- 2 T. cherry Jello mix, dry
- 1/2 tsp. almond extract
- 2 11oz. cans cherry pie filling

directions:

Combine water, sugar, cornstarch, salt, jello and almond extract over medium heat till thick. Remove from heat and cool 5-10 min. Stir in pie filling. Fill crust and top with 2nd crust. Dot with butter and a generous amount of sugar. Bake at 375° for 45-55 min. till golden and crispy.

Millionaire Pie

ingredients:

2 9" graham cracker pie crust

1/2 cup whipped cream
1 can sweetened condensed milk
1 can crushed pineapple, drained
Juice of 1 lemon

directions:

Combine all the ingredients in a bowl and pour into two graham cracker pie crusts. Put in the refrigerator and chill. Enjoy.

Old Fashioned Butter Cake

ingredients:

- 3 cups all-purpose flour
- 1 tsp. baking powder
- 1 tsp. salt
- 1/2 tsp. baking soda
- 1 cup butter
- 2 cups sugar
- 4 eggs
- 1 cup buttermilk or cream
- 2 tsp. vanilla extract

directions:

Preheat oven to 350°. Grease and flour 9x13 pan or bundt pan. Sift together flour, baking powder, baking soda, and salt, set aside. Cream together butter, sugar, mix in eggs and vanilla. Blend in buttermilk. Fold in dry ingredients. Pour into prepared pan and bake for about 1 hour or until toothpick comes out clean. Let cool completely.

Ice with Butter Cream Frosting on the next page (p.127).

Butter Cream Frosting

ingredients:

- 1 cup butter softened
- 1/2 cup milk or cream
- 2 tsp. vanilla extract
- 5 cups powdered sugar

directions:

Cream butter and vanilla until smooth, add sugar. Mix in milk a little at a time, blend well until desired consistency. Spread onto take and serve.

Heavenly Spice Cake

ingredients:

    1/2 cup shortening
    1 1/2 cup sugar
    1 egg
    3 T. Cocoa
    1/2 tsp. cloves
    1/4 tsp. baking soda
    1/2 tsp. cinnamon
    1/2 tsp. salt
    1 t. vanilla
    1 cup buttermilk
    1 1/2 cup flour

Filling:
    1 cup chopped nuts
    1 cup sugar
    1/2 cup cream
    1 egg
    1 tsp. vanilla

directions:

Sift all your dry ingredients. Beat shortening, sugar, egg, vanilla, and buttermilk. Fold in dry ingredients. Bake at 350° until toothpick comes out clean.

Mix all the filling ingredients together and cook until thick. Let cool and spread over cake. Enjoy.

Lemon Cake

ingredients:

    1 pkg. lemon cake mix
    1 pkg. large lemon pudding mix
    1 can apricot nectar (shake well)
    4 eggs
    1/2 cup oil

Glaze:
    3 T. lemon juice
    1 cup powdered sugar

directions:

Mix well and bake in greased and floured bundt pan. Turn out on cake plate or carrier.

Mix the lemon juice and powdered sugar. Brush on hot cake.

Orange Glazed Cake

ingredients:

1 cup sugar
1/2 cup shortening
2 eggs
3/4 cup sour milk
1 tsp. baking soda
1 tsp. vanilla
2 cups flour
1 cup raisins
1 orange peel zest

Glaze:
Juice of one orange
1/2 cup sugar

directions:

In large bowl beat sugar, eggs, and vanilla until light and fluffy. Add in shortening and sour milk and mix well. Fold in flour, baking soda, raisins, and orange zest. Pour into greased floured bundt pan. Bake at 350° for 45 min to 1 hour. While cake is baking make your glaze. Beat the juice of one orange with 1/2 cup sugar and set aside. Turn out the cake while still warm onto serving platter. Pour the glaze onto the cake while still warm. Enjoy.

Dream Cake with Icing

ingredients:

Cake:
- 2 cups sugar
- 1 stick butter
- 1/2 Crisco
- 5 egg separated
- 2 cup flour
- 1 tsp. baking soda
- 1 cup coconut

Icing:
- 1 block cream cheese
- 1 stick butter
- 1 box powdered sugar
- 1 cup nuts
- 1 tsp. vanilla

directions:

Sift flour and baking soda. Beat egg yolks, sugar, butter, Crisco. Mix in coconut and sifted ingredients. Beat egg whites and fold into the cake mixture. Bake at 350° for 25 min or until done. Makes 3 layered rounds.

Beat cream cheese, butter, and vanilla until light and fluffy. Mix in powdered sugar and nuts. Spread over cake. Enjoy.

Fruit Cocktail Cake

ingredients:

1/4 lb. margarine (1 stick of margarine)
1 1/3 cup sugar
2 eggs
1 cup chopped nuts
1 can fruit cocktail
2 heaping cups flour
2 tsp. baking soda
2 tsp. vanilla

directions:

Mix margarine, sugar, eggs, and vanilla. Add and mix flour. Fold in fruit cocktail, juice and all. Add nuts. Sprinkle the top with 1 1/2 cup brown sugar. Bake in 9x13 pan at 350° for 40-45 min. serve cold or warm with whipped cream.

Strawberry Cake with Icing

ingredients:

Cake:
- 1 box white cake mix
- 1 box frozen strawberries
- 1 box jello strawberry mix
- 4 eggs
- 1 cup oil
- 1 cup coconut
- 1 cup pecans

Icing:
- 1 box powdered sugar
- 1 stick butter
- 1/2 cup pecans
- 1/2 cup strawberries

directions:

Mix everything and pour into prepared pan. Bake at 350° for 20-25 min or until done. Cool completely before removing from pan.

Mix powdered sugar, butter. Stir in pecans and strawberries. Spread onto cooled cake. Top with fresh whole strawberries.

Carrot Cake with Cream Cheese Frosting

ingredients:

    3 cups flour
    2 cups sugar
    2 cups grated carrots
    1 1/2 cups chopped pecans
    1 ½ cup oil
    1 can crushed pineapple and juice
    Pinch of salt
    3 eggs
    2 tsp. baking powder
    1 tsp. baking soda
    1 tsp. cinnamon
    2 tsp. vanilla

Frosting:
    1 block cream cheese
    1 stick butter
    1 box powdered sugar
    1 cup chopped pecans
    1 tsp. vanilla

directions:

Sift dry ingredients and mix. Beat eggs, vanilla, oil, and sugar. Add in carrots, pineapple and the juice, and pecans. Fold in dry ingredients. Pour into greased and floured pan. Bake at 350° for 1 hour to 1 1/2 hours.

Beat cream cheese, butter, and vanilla until light and fluffy. Mix in powdered sugar and nuts. Spread over cooled carrot cake. Enjoy.

Mexican Wedding Cake

ingredients:

Cake:
- 2 cups sugar
- 2 cups flour
- 1 tsp. baking soda
- 1 tsp. vanilla
- 1 20 oz can crushed pineapple with juice
- ½ cup pecans

Icing:
- 1 stick margarine melted
- 1 8 oz cream cheese
- 3/4 cup sugar
- 1/2 tsp. vanilla
- 1/2 cup chopped pecans

directions:

Mix together and bake at 350° for 30 minutes, in a 9x13 pan, greased and floured.

Beat the icing ingredients until stiff and fluffy. Add pecans and vanilla. Put on cake while still warm.

Sopapilla Cheesecake

ingredients:

- 2 tubes crescent rolls
- 2 8 oz. blocks cream cheese softened
- 1 cup sugar
- Splash vanilla
- 4 T. melted butter
- 1/2 cup sugar
- Cinnamon

directions:

Spray a 9x13 baking dish, unroll one tube of crescent rolls on bottom. In a bowl beat cream cheese, sugar, and vanilla until light and fluffy. Spread cream cheese mixture over the crescent rolls. Top with the other tube of crescent rolls. Drizzle the melted butter over the top, and sprinkle sugar and cinnamon on top. Bake at 350° for 30-40 min or until golden brown.

Potato Cake

ingredients:

- 1 cup butter
- 2 cups sugar
- 3 cups flour
- 1/3 cup cocoa
- 1/2 cup sweetened condensed milk
- 1 cup mashed potatoes
- 1 cup nuts
- 3 eggs
- 1 tsp. vanilla
- 2 tsp. cinnamon
- 1/2 tsp. allspice
- 1 tsp. baking powder

directions:

Wash, peel, boil and mash potatoes, set aside. Sift flour, cocoa, baking powder and spices. Mix butter, sugar, eggs, and vanilla. Mix in mashed potatoes to wet ingredients. Fold in dry ingredients and nuts. Pour into prepared pan and bake at 350° till toothpick comes out clean. Enjoy.

7-Up Pound Cake

ingredients:

- 1 cup butter
- 1/2 cup Crisco
- 3 cups sugar
- 3 cups flour
- 5 eggs
- 1 1/4 cup 7-Up room temp (not Diet)
- 2 tsp. lemon extract
- 2 tsp. almond extract

directions:

Cream butter, Crisco and sugar well. Beat in eggs. Beat in flour. Fold in 7-Up and extracts. Bake in greased and floured bundt pan at 350° about 2 hours or until toothpick comes out clean.

Pound Cake

ingredients:

- 2 sticks butter
- 2 cups sugar
- 6 eggs
- 2 cups flour
- 1 tsp. baking powder
- 1 can coconut milk
- 1 tsp. vanilla
- 1 tsp. salt

directions:

Cream butter and sugar well. Beat in eggs, vanilla, and coconut milk. Beat in flour, salt, and baking powder. Bake in greased and floured bundt pan at 350° about 1 1/2 hours or until toothpick comes out clean.

Chocolate Chip Pound Cake

ingredients:

- 1 box yellow cake mix
- 1/2 cup oil
- 2 small pkg. instant chocolate pudding mix
- 1 1/2 cup water
- 12 oz chocolate chips
- 1 cool whip tub

directions:

Beat well and fold in 12 oz chocolate chips. Pour into a greased and floured bundt pan. Bake at 350° for 1 1/2 hour. Serve with a dallop of cool whip.

Pudding Cake

ingredients/directions:

In a 9x13 pan mix:
- 1 cup flour
- 1 stick butter
- 1 cup chopped pecans

Make sure to really get this all mixed together and patted gently. Bake at 350° for 20 minutes.

Mix:
- 8 oz cream cheese, room temp
- 1 cup powdered sugar
- 1 cup cool whip, out a large tub of cool whip

Plop small spoonfulls all over the cooled crust. Spread evenly, but never lift the spoon or the crust will come with it.

Mix until thick:
- 1 small pkg. instant vanilla pudding mix
- 1 small pkg. instant chocolate pudding mix
- 2 cups milk

Spread over the cream cheese mixture. Spread the rest of the cool whip over the top of everything. Grate a Hearshy bar over the top. Chill and serve.

Pumpkin Cake

ingredients:

- 3 cups flour
- 3 cups sugar
- 3 eggs
- 1 cup oil
- 1 tsp. vanilla
- 1 tsp. cloves
- 1 tsp. nutmeg
- 1 tsp. cinnamon
- 1/2 tsp. baking powder
- 1 tsp. baking soda
- 1 can pumpkin

directions:

Beat well and bake in greased floured bundt pan at 350° for 1 hr. 15 min. Until done.

Zucchini Cake

ingredients:

- 3 cups grated zucchini
- 3 cups sugar
- 1 1/2 cups oil
- 4 eggs
- 3 cups flour
- 2 tsp. baking soda
- 2 tsp. baking powder
- 1 1/2 tsp cinnamon
- 1/2 tsp. salt
- 1 cup chopped pecans

directions:

Mix together in order given. Bake in a greased and floured loaf pan at 300° for 1 – 1 1/2 hours.

Poppy Seed Cake

ingredients:

    1 box yellow cake mix
    1/4 cup poppy seeds
    1/2 cup sugar
    2/3 cup oil
    8 oz. sour cream
    4 eggs

directions:

Mix all ingredients in a large bowl. Then pour into a greased and floured bundt pan. Bake at 350° for 45 min or until done. Once cooled turn out onto a platter. Enjoy.

Dump Cake

ingredients:

- 1 can crushed pineapple
- 1 can cherry pie filling
- 1 box yellow cake mix
- 1 1/2 sticks butter, melted
- 1/2 cups chopped nuts

directions:

Grease 9x13 pan. Dump in pineapple and spread evenly. Now cherry pie filling. Now dry cake mix. Now nuts. Drizzle melted butter over all of it. Bake at 350° about 1 hour until brown.

Coconut Icing

ingredients:

3/4 cup coconut milk
1 cup sugar
Grated coconut

directions:

Boil coconut milk and sugar for 5 min stirring constantly. Remove from heat and mix in grated coconut. Let cool. Spread onto cake or inbetween layers. Always moist and juicy.

Cream Frosting

ingredients:

1/2 cup butter melted
1 cup brown sugar
1/2 milk
1 1/2 cup or more powdered sugar

directions:

Melt butter and add in brown sugar. Heat over low heat stirring constantly. Add milk and bring to boiling point. Remove from heat and add powdered sugar, beat well. Spread over cake.

Molasses Cookies

ingredients:

Mix:
    3/4 cup shortening
    1 egg
    1 cup sugar
    1/4 cup molasses

Sift and stir in:
    2 tsp. baking soda
    1/4 tsp salt
    3/4 tsp cloves
    1 tsp cinnamon
    3/4 tsp ginger
    2 cups flour

directions:

Mix thoroughly. Form into small balls about the size of walnuts. Place 2" apart onto greased pan. Bake at 350° for 10 min or until firm but soft. Once baked, roll or top with powdered sugar, while still warm. Makes 4-5 dozen.

Pumpkin Cookies

ingredients:

Mix:
- 1 cup butter softened
- 3 cups sugar
- 1 can pumpkin
- 2 eggs
- 2 tsp. vanilla

Sift and combine in bowl:
- 5 cups flour
- 2 tsp. baking soda
- 2 tsp baking powder
- 2 tsp. cinnamon
- 1 tsp. nutmeg
- 1 tsp. salt

directions:

Cream butter and sugar in large bowl. Add pumpkin and vanilla. Beat till light and creamy. Mix in dry ingredients. Drop by rounded tablespoon on greased cookie sheet. Bake at 350° for 20 min. Cool completely. Glaze.

Glaze: Combine 1 box powdered sugar (4 cups), 6 T. milk, 2 T. melted butter and 2 tsp. vanilla.

Easy Peanut Butter Cookies

ingredients:

- 1 can sweetened condensed milk
- 3/4 cup peanut butter
- 2 cup Bisquick
- 1 tsp. vanilla

directions:

Preheat oven to 375°. In large mixer bowl beat sweetened condensed milk and peanut butter until smooth. Add Bisquick and vanilla, mix well. Shape into 1" balls roll in sugar. Place 2" apart on ungreased pan. Flatten with fork. Bake 6-8 min. until lightly browned. Do not overbake. Cool. Store in tightly closed container at room temp.

Peanut Butter Blossom Cookies

ingredients:

1 can sweetened condensed milk
3/4 cup peanut butter
2 cup Bisquick
1 tsp. vanilla
Chocolate kiss candies

directions:

Preheat oven to 375°. In large mixer bowl beat sweetened condensed milk and peanut butter until smooth. Add Bisquick and vanilla, mix well. Shape into 1" balls roll in sugar. Place 2" apart on ungreased pan. Bake 6-8 min. or until lightly browned. When done baking press a chocolate kiss candy in the center of each cookie while still warm. Cool. Store in tightly closed container at room temp.

Peanut Butter Cookies

ingredients:

- 1/2 cup shortening
- 1/2 cup peanut butter
- 1 cup sugar
- 2 eggs
- 2 cups flour
- 1 tsp. baking powder
- 1/2 tsp. baking soda
- 1/2 tsp. salt

directions:

Preheat to 375°. In large bowl beat eggs, and sugar. Add in peanut butter and shortening mix until smooth. Mix in flour, baking powder, baking soda, and salt. Shape into 1" balls, place 2" apart on ungreased pan. Using a fork press each cookie ball flat. Bake 6-8 min. or until lightly browned. Cool. Store in tightly closed container at room temp.

Guess Again Cookies

ingredients:

- 1 cup margarine
- 2 cups flour
- 1/2 cup crunched potato chips
- 1/2 cup sugar
- 1 tsp. vanilla
- 1/2 cup chopped nuts

directions:

Cream margarine, sugar, and vanilla. Add potato chips and nuts. Stir with spoon. Stir in flour. Form into balls and place on ungreased pan. Press flat with bottom of glass dipped in sugar. Bake at 350° 15-18 min. till lightly browned.

Sugar Cookies

ingredients:

- 1 cup butter room temp
- 1 cup sugar
- 2 eggs
- 2 tsp. almond extract
- 3 1/4 cup flour
- 1/2 tsp. baking soda
- 1/2 tsp. baking powder
- 1/2 tsp. salt

directions:

Cream butter and sugar. Add eggs and almond extract. Mix well. Add all the dry ingredients. Bake at 350° for 6-8 min.

Simple Sugar Cookies

ingredients:

    1/2 cup butter
    1 cup sugar
    2 eggs
    1 T. cream
    2 1/4 cups flour
    1 1/2 tsp. baking powder
    1/2 tsp. nutmeg
    1/4 tsp. salt

directions:

Cream butter and sugar. Add eggs and cream, mix well. Add all the dry ingredients. Bake at 350° for 6-8 min.

Unbaked Chocolate Oatmeal Cookies

ingredients:

    1 cups sugar
    1 cup milk
    6 T. cocoa
    1 stick butter
Bring everything above to a boil for 3 min. Remove from heat.

    1 cup peanut butter
    1 box rolled oats
    1 tsp. vanilla

directions:

Bring everything to a boil for 3 min. Remove from heat. Stir in the peanut butter. Stir in rolled oats and vanilla. Drop on wax paper and let sit for 5 min. Enjoy.

Cocoa Oatmeal Cookies

ingredients:

- 2 cups sugar
- 1/2 cup cocoa
- 1/2 cup butter
- 1/2 cup milk
- 3 cups rolled oats
- 1 tsp. vanilla
- Pinch of salt

directions:

In a large bowl mix all the ingredients together and form 1" balls, place 2" apart on a greased cookie sheet. Bake at 350°. Makes 40 cookies.

other desserts

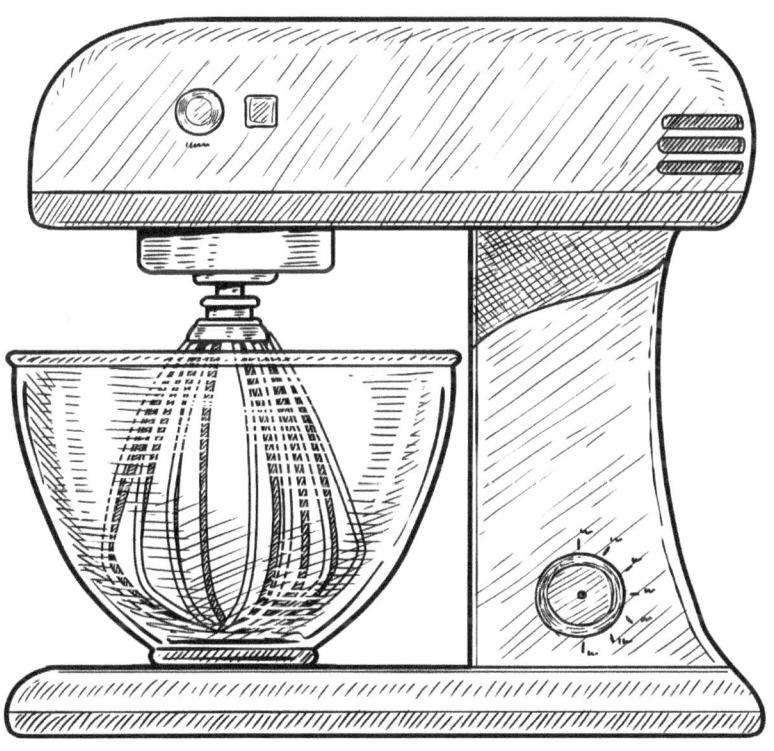

Fresh Fruit Salad

ingredients:

Grapes
Strawberries
Bananas
Mandarin oranges
Blueberries
Apples
Peacans
1 1/2 cups heavy whipping cream
Sugar

directions:

Clean and prepare all fruits. In a bowl beat heavy whipping cream and sugar, to taste, until thick, stiff and creamy, you need to be able to form peaks. Fold in the fruit and nuts and enjoy.

Peach Cobbler

ingredients:

8 fresh peaches peeled, pitted, and sliced
1 cup sugar
1/2 tsp. cinnamon
1 cup water

Cake topping:
2 cups flour
1/2 cup sugar
1/2 cup packed brown sugar
2 tsp. baking powder
1 tsp. salt
12 T. cold butter cut into small pieces

directions:

In pot mix peaches, sugar, cinnamon, and water then simmer for 5-10 min. Mix all cake ingredients together adding butter slowly. Then add 1 cup of juice from simmering peaches to mix. Put all peaches and juice into 9x13 then spoon cake mix over it. Sprinkle with sugar. Bake at 400° for 30 min.

Fried Doughnuts

ingredients:

2 cans of ready biscuits
Oil
Powdered sugar
Sugar
Cinnamon
Cocoa powder
Sewing thimble, or small cookie cutter

directions:

Get a medium size sauce pot and pour enough oil to fry your doughnuts. Turn the heat onto medium high. Arrange 3 different plates for your toppings. One plate mix sugar and cinnamon, another plate plain powdered sugar, and the last plate powdered sugar with cocoa powder. Open your cans of biscuits and lay them out flat. Using your thimble, or small cookie cutter, cut out a small circle in the center of your biscuits. Set the small circle aside, don't discard. Once you have all the circles cut out you can start frying your dough. Cook on one side till golden brown, then flip and cook the other side till golden brown. Remove from the oil and cover with your choice of topping. Repeat until all the dough is cooked. Do the same process for all the small circles of dough, creating doughnut holes. Enjoy.

Quick Cherry Cobbler

ingredients:

    1 can cherries
    1 cup sugar
    2 cups water
Bring to a boil.

Mix:
    1 cup sugar
    1 cup flour
    1 tsp. baking powder
    1/2 cup milk

directions:

Melt 1/4 lb. margarin (1 stick) in baking dish. Pour in cake mixture. Add fruit mixture last and bake at 450° till done.

Slow Cooker Cinnamon Nuts

ingredients:

- 1 1/4 cup sugar
- 1 1/4 cup brown sugar
- 3 T. cinnamon
- 1 egg white
- 2 tsp. vanilla
- 3 cups nuts
- 1/4 cup water
- 1/8 tsp salt

directions:

Mix sugar, brown sugar, cinnamon, and salt. Whisk egg white and vanilla till frothy. Coat the nuts. Place in slow cooker. Add dry ingredients, mix well. Cook on low for 3-4 hours. In the last hour add 1/4 cup water stir every 20 min. take out and spread on wax paper to cool. Enjoy.

Carmel Popcorn

ingredients:

Boil 5 Minuets:
- 1 cup margarine
- 1/4 cup white syrup
- 2 cup brown sugar

Add:
- 1/2 tsp. baking soda
- 1 tsp. salt
- 1 tsp. vanilla

directions:

Pour immediately over 8 qts. of popped corn and stir gently to coat in large, greased roaster pan. Mix well. Bake uncovered at 250° for 1 hour, stirring every 15 min.

Candied Grapes

ingredients:

- 1-2 lbs any color grapes
- 1-2 boxes grape jello mix

directions:

Wash grapes and place into ziplock bag still wet. Add jello mix and shake, make sure to cover all the grapes in the jello mix. Pour out onto cooking sheet and set in fridge till the jello mix hardens. Enjoy.

Raspberry Fluff

ingredients/directions:

Combine in mixing bowl and let stand 15 to 20 minutes.
- 8 1/2 can crushed pineapple
- 3 oz. pkg. raspberry Jello mix

Then add:
- 1 cup small curd cottage cheese

Fold in:
- 1/2 cup chopped pecans
- 8 oz. cool whip

Set in refrigerator till ready to serve.

Banana Pudding

ingredients:

- 8 oz cream cheese
- 14 oz can sweetened condensed milk
- Splash of vanilla
- 8 oz cool whip tub
- 3 cups milk
- 2 3.4 oz instant vanilla pudding mix
- 1 box mini vanilla wafer cookies
- 4 large bananas sliced

directions:

Whip cream cheese until fluffy, add sweetened condensed milk, and vanilla; whip again. Fold in whip topping, set aside. Combine milk and pudding in large bowl using electric mixer for about 3 min. fold cream cheese mixture into pudding. Layer cookies, sliced bananas, and pudding till gone. Cover and refrigerate 3-4 hours or until set. Top with cool whip desire.

Strawberry Banana Salad

ingredients:

- 1 box banana-strawberry Jello mix
- 1 cup hot water
- 1 box strawberries
- 1 banana
- 1/2 carton sour cream
- 1/4 cup chopped nuts

directions:

Mix hot water into the Jello mix, along with the strawberries. Chill for 30 min. Add one banana sliced up, sour cream and nuts to the Jello mixture, let set in ice box for 2 to 3 hours. Enjoy.

Holiday Marshmallows

ingredients:

   1 pkg. jumbo marshmallows
   1 box decorative toothpicks
   2 boxes instant Jello mix

*Change your color Jello mix to match the holiday your celebrating.
Christmas- green mix and red mix
Thanksgiving- orange mix and yellow mix
Easter- yellow mix and green mix
Halloween- orange mix and yellow mix

directions:

Dip the ends of the marshmallows into bowl of water the moisten, then into the Jello mix of your choice. Keep them uncovered until completely dried then add your decorative toothpick to the top and serve on
platter.

Oreo Balls

ingredients:

- 1 package Oreos (any flavor regular, mint, etc.)
- 1 block cream cheese
- 1 package white chocolate chips
- 1 package milk chocolate chips

directions:

Place all oreo cookies into food processor and chop finely. Place in bowl, using hands combine cream cheese evenly. Make into 1" balls till gone. Place in freezer for 10-20 min. Melt white chocolate chips and dip oreo balls into the chocolate, let harden on wax paper. Melt milk chocolate and drizzle over chocolate covered oreo balls. Refrigerate.

Peanut Patties

ingredients:

3 cups raw peanuts
1 1/2 cup can milk
1 1/2 tsp. vanilla
4 1/2 cups sugar
1 cup white Karo
3 T. margarine

directions:

Mix all together and cook until soft ball forms in cold water. Add in food coloring. Beat until thick. Drop on wax paper.

Buckeyes

ingredients:

- 4 sticks butter, softened
- 4 cups peanut butter
- 3 lbs. powdered sugar
- 24 oz. chocolate chips
- 1 bar paraffin

directions:

Mix butter, peanut butter and powdered sugar. Shape in balls. Refrigerate. Melt chocolate chips and paraffin. Dip balls into chocolate mixture. Cool on wax paper.

Haystacks

ingredients:

- 12 oz butterscotch chips
- 1 small can chow mein noodles
- 1 cup salted peanuts

directions:

Melt chips in microwave exactly by pkg. directions. Mix in noodles and peanut. Drop on wax paper.

Date and Nut Roll Candy

ingredients:

- 1 1/3 cups sugar
- 2/3 cup evaporated milk
- 2/3 cup finely chopped dates
- 2/3 cup salted peanuts or pecans
- 3/4 tsp. vanilla
- 1/2 cup unsalted nuts

directions:

Mix all the ingredients except for the unsalted nuts and roll into a log, Place the log onto serving platter. Pack the unsalted nuts on top of the loaf. Slice and serve.

Crockpot Apple Butter

ingredients:

6 cups canned applesauce, drained
3 cups sugar
1/3 cups apple cider vinegar
2 T. cinnamon
1/4 tsp. cloves

directions:

Mix all ingredients and cook in slow cooker on high for 4 hours. Then turn on low for 4 hours. Stir throughout the process, careful not to let it burn. Makes about 4 pints.

Never Fail Peanut Butter

ingredients:

- 3 cups sugar
- 1 cup white karo syrup
- 1/2 cup water

directions:

Cook until threads. Add 2 cups of peanuts and cook until golden brown. Then add 3 T. butter, 2 tsp. baking soda, and 1/2 tsp. salt. Pour into butter dish to cool. Enjoy.

breads

Pumpkin Bread

ingredients:

2 sticks margarin
2 3/4 cup sugar
3 eggs
3 1/2 cup flour
1 tsp. cinnamon
1 tsp. nutmeg
1 tsp. cloves
1 tsp. baking soda
2 tsp. baking powder
1 can pumpkin
1 tsp vanilla
1 cup chopped nuts

directions:

Cream margarine, sugar well, add eggs, spices and vanilla. Mix flour, baking soda, and baking powder together. Add pumpkin and flour mixture to sugar mixture, mixing well. Add nuts. Pour/spoon into 3 coffee cans or loaf pans. Bake at 325° for 1–1 1/2 hrs. Good with butter or whipped cream.

Candied Nut Topped Banana Bread

ingredients:

Muffins:
- 3-4 large ripe bananas
- 3/4 cup sugar
- 1 egg
- 1/3 cup oil
- 1 1/2 cup flour
- 1 tsp. baking soda
- 1 tsp. baking powder
- 1/2 tsp. salt
- 1/2 tsp all spice
- 1tsp. cinnamon
- Splash of vanilla
- 3/4 cup chopped pecans

Candied Nut Topping:
- 3/4 cup copped pecans
- 2 T. brown sugar
- 1 T. melted butter

directions:

Mash bananas, mix in sugar and egg till well blended. Add oil and mix well. Add vanilla. In separate bowl sift flour, baking powder, baking soda, salt, cinnamon, nutmeg and add in nuts. Add wet ingredients mix until wet, don't over mix. In separate bowl mix brown sugar, nuts, and melted butter until all nuts are coated. Spoon batter in greased or lined muffin pan and top with a spoon full of coated nuts. Bake at 350° for 20-25 min or until done.

Beer Biscuits

ingredients:

    4 cups Bisquick
    1 can beer (room temp)
    1/4 cup oil
    1/2 tsp. salt
    2 T. sugar

directions:

Drop in well greased muffin tins. Bake at 350° until done. Makes 24 rolls.

Biscuits

ingredients:

- 1 cup flour
- 1/2 tsp. baking soda
- 4 1/4 tsp. salt
- 1 tsp. baking powder
- 3 T. shortening
- 1/2 cup buttermilk

directions:

Sift the dry ingredients and mix in the wet ingredients. Plop dough balls onto greased pan and bake at 350° until golden brown on top. Top with melted butter. Enjoy.

Christmas Morning Rolls

ingredients:

- 1 pkg. frozen dinner rolls, need 24
- 1 box 3.5 oz butterscotch pudding (NOT instant mix)
- 1 cup brown sugar
- 1/4 cup sugar
- 1 tsp. cinnamon
- 1/2 cup chopped pecans
- 1/2 cup melted butter

directions:

Grease bundt pan. Place frozen rolls in pan. Mix brown sugar, and pudding mix and sprinkle over rolls. Mix sugar and cinnamon, sprinkle on. Sprinkle on chopped pecans. Pour melted butter over all of it. Leave on counter overnight. Do not cover. Bake at 350° for 30-40 min. or until done. Let sit 15 min. Carefully invert onto platter. Enjoy.

Holiday Morning French Toast

ingredients:

- 1 cup brown sugar
- 1/2 cup melted butter
- 3 tsp. cinnamon
- 3 granny smith apples peeled and thinly sliced
- 1/2 cup raisins, or dried cranberries
- 1 loaf Italian or French bread, sliced 1" thick
- 6 eggs
- 1 1/2 cup milk
- 1 T. vanilla

directions:

Combine brown sugar, butter and 1 tsp. cinnamon in 9x13 pan. Add apples and rains, coat well. Spread evenly. Arrange bread slices on top. Mix eggs, milk, vanilla and 2 tsp. cinnamon. Pour over bread. Cover and refrigerate overnight. Bake covered with foil at 375° for 40 min. Uncover and bake 5 more min. Let stand 5 min. Serve warm.

Cornbread

ingredients:

    1/2 cup flour
    1 cup corn meal
    1/2 tsp. baking soda
    1/2 tsp. salt
    1 cup buttermilk
    1 egg

directions:

Mix all ingredients together and pour into greased cast iron pan and bake at 350° until golden brown.

Savory Party Bread

ingredients:

- 1 lb. sourdough loaf of bread
- 1 lb. Monterey jack cheese, sliced
- 1/2 cup butter melted
- 1/2 cup chopped green onions
- 2-3 tsp. poppy seeds

directions:

Cut bread length wise and crosswise, without cutting through the loaf. (Make cross hatch marks on the top) insert cheese slices between cuts. Combine butter, onions and poppy seeds. Drizzle over bread. Wrap in foil. Place on baking sheet. Bake at 350° for 15 minutes covered with foil. Bake 10 more minutes uncovered or until cheese completely melts.

Pumpkin Chocolate Chip Muffins

ingredients:

1 2/3 cup flour
1 cup sugar
1 T. cinnamon
1/2 tsp. all spice
1 tsp baking soda
1 tsp. baking powder
1/4 tsp salt
2 eggs
1 can pumpkin
1 cup melted butter
1 cup semi-sweet chocolate chips
Splash of vanilla

directions:

Mix all dry ingredients and chocolate chips. Combine melted butter, pumpkin, eggs and vanilla in separate bowl. Combine dry ingredients into wet, fold don't mix. Spoon into greased or lined muffin pans. Bake at 350° for 15-20 min or until done. Makes 18 muffins.

Ever Ready Raisin Bran Muffins

ingredients:

- 1 15-20 oz box Raisin Bran cereal
- 5 cups flour
- 2 cups sugar
- 1 cup brown sugar
- 5 tsp. baking soda
- 1 tsp. salt
- 4 eggs beaten
- 1 qt. buttermilk
- 1 cup oil

directions:

In large bowl combine all dry ingredients including cereal. Add eggs, oil and buttermilk. Mix well. Cover and store batter in refrigerator up to one month. Bake as needed in a greased muffin pan at 350° to 400° for about 30 min.

*The batter can be stored in the refrigerator covered for up to 1 month.

Hot Spiced Tea Mix

ingredients:

1 cup instant tea
2 cups sugar
1 pkg. instant sweetened lemonade
1 cup Tang
3/4 tsp. cinnamon
1/4 tsp. cloves

directions:

Add 2-3 tsp. of the mix into a mug of hot water. Stir and enjoy!

Hot Peach Tea Mix

ingredients:

- 4 boxes peach Jello mix
- 1 cup Tang
- 1 cup instant tea
- 1 pkg. instant sweetened lemonade

directions:

Add 2-3 tsp. of the mix into a mug of hot water. Stir and enjoy!

Party Punch

ingredients:

    Orange juice
    Pineapple juice
    Cranberry juice
    Tea – weakened
    Sugar to taste

directions:

Mix all the ingredients in a large punch bowl, chill and serve.

Soda Punch

ingredients:

    1 can pineapple chunks with the juice
    1 qt Cream Soda or Canada Dry
    Few scoops of vanilla ice cream

directions:

In a large punch bowl mix your soda, pinapple chunks and the juice. Add as many scoops of vanilla ice cream as you want and let them float. Enjoy.

Kool-Aid Punch

ingredients:

1 46 oz can pineapple with the juice
1 pkg. Lemon Lime Kool-Aid
1 pt. water, or more as needed
1 cup sugar

directions:

Mix all the ingredients in a large punch bowl, add ice and serve.

Rainbow Sherbet Punch

ingredients:

- 2 liter Sprite or Sierra Mist
- 1/2 gallon Hawaiin Punch
- 1/2 gallon Rainbow Sherbet ice cream

directions:

Mix the Sprite and Hawaiin Punch together in a large punch bowl. Top with Rainbow Sherbet ice cream and serve.

Pear Preserve Wine

ingredients:

- 2 gallons peeled pears
- 1 gallon sugar
- 2 lemons sliced

directions:

Put everything into large stock pot and cover with water, simmer around 6 hours. Cool and strain.

Pina Colada Punch

ingredients:

- 1 can coconut cream
- 4 6 oz. cans pineapple juice
- 1 2 liter bottle club soda
- 1/2 gallon pineapple Sherbet ice cream

directions:

Mix the coconut cream, pineapple juice and club soda together in a large punch bowl. Top with pineapple Sherbet ice cream and serve.

canning

Bread and Butter Pickles

ingredients:

- 2 qt. cucumbers sliced
- 2 T. salt
- 2 medium onions
- 1 tsp. mustard seed
- 1 tsp. celery seed
- 1 tsp. turmeric seed
- 2 cups vinegar
- 2 cups sugar
- 1/2 cups brown sugar

directions:

Clean and slice your cucumbers. Put into bowl and cover with water and add salt. Let that sit in the water and salt for about 24 hours. Drain and add the remaining ingredients. Simmer on low for about 30 minutes. Divide cucumbers and brine into jars and seal.

Relish

ingredients:

    1 qt. green tomatoes
    1 qt. onions
    1 qt. cabbage
    1 qt. red or green bell peppers
    1 qt. celery
    1 qt. sugar
    1 qt. vinegar
    2 T. flour
    2 T. salt
    2 T. turmeric
    2 T. dry mustard

directions:

Dice tomatoes, onions, cabbage, bell peppers, and celery. Mix all ingredients into large pot and cook for 45 minutes. Divide evenly into jars and seal.

Chow-Chow

ingredients:

14 lbs. tomatoes
7 lbs. cabbage
25 onions
1 qt. vinegar
3 cups sugar
1 tsp. cinnamon

1 tsp. allspice

directions:

Dice up tomatoes, cabbage, and onions. Mix in large pot with remaining ingredients. Cook slowly until well done. Divide up into jars and seal.

Squash Relish

ingredients:

- 12 cups squash shredded or diced (yellow or green)
- 2 bell peppers
- 5 T. salt
- 4 cups onion
- 1 jar pimento

Drain the ingredients above by putting them into a colander and let stand overnight.

The sauce:
- 2 1/2 cups white vinegar
- 5 cups sugar
- 2 T. pickling spice
- 1 tsp. turmeric
- 1 tsp. celery seeds

directions:

Put all of the spices in a mesh bag, and place the bag in a pot to boil. Remove the spice bag. Add squash mixture and boil again. Seal in jars. Makes about 3 quarts.

Sandwhich Spread

ingredients:

    2 qts. green tomatoes diced
    1 qt. onions chopped
    1 qt. cabbage chopped
    1 qt. sweet peppers chopped
    1 gallon water
    1 cup salt

Add all the ingredients above and soak for 4 hours and drain.

Add:
    2 qt. vinegar
    1 pt. sugar
    1 cup flour
    6 T. dry mustard
    1 T. turmeric powder

directions:

Cook everything together for 20 min. Evenly distribute the mixture into canning jars and seal.

Grape Jam

ingredients:

- 5 cups grapes sliced
- 1 can Welches grape juice
- 5 cups sugar
- 1 box sure jell

directions:

Cook grapes with small amount of water and turn through strainer. Add Welches grape juice. Add sugar and box of sure jell according to the box instructions. Divide evenly and seal.

www.ingramcontent.com/pod-product-compliance
Lightning Source LLC
Chambersburg PA
CBHW061147170426
43209CB00011B/1581